GRIDIRON GREATS:

8 OF TODAY'S HOTTEST NFL STARS

Ashley Jude Collie

Sports Illustrated
KIDS
B O O K S

This Library Edition First Published and Exclusively Distributed by
The Rosen Publishing Group, Inc.
New York

This library edition first published in 2003 and exclusively distributed by
The Rosen Publishing Group, Inc., New York

Copyright © SPORTS ILLUSTRATED FOR KIDS Books

Book Design: Michelle Innes
Additional editorial material: Nel Yomtov

Photo Credits: Cover (left), p. 19 © Icon SMI; cover (middle), p. 61 © Al Messerschmidt/Icon
SMI; cover (right), pp. 75, 83 © Icon Sports Media; all background images © Photodisc; p. 7,
© Drew Hallowell/Icon SMI; p. 29 © John Grieshop/Icon SMI; p. 41 © John Biever/SI/Icon
SMI; p. 51 © John McDonough/SI/Icon SMI

First edition

>> CONTENTS

>> INTRODUCTION

Every Sunday, amazing things happen in the NFL. A gutsy quarterback leads his team on a clutch drive to win the game in the final seconds. A running back busts through a hole in the defensive line and zooms off on a long, electrifying run downfield. A wide receiver soars above desperate defenders to pluck a touchdown pass out of the sky. A ferocious defender makes a bone-crunching, helmet-rattling, game-saving tackle or sack. There's always something for football fans to cheer their lungs out about.

Gridiron Greats: 8 of Today's Hottest NFL Stars tells the stories of eight players who make exciting things happen on the gridiron week after week, season after season. You'll meet a fantastic quartet of quarterbacks: Kurt Warner of the St. Louis Rams, Drew Bledsoe of the New England Patriots, Steve McNair of the Tennessee Titans, and Brett Favre of the Green Bay Packers. You'll read about a dynamic duo of running backs: Marshall Faulk of the

Rams and Eddie George of the Titans. You'll thrill to the exploits of gravity–defying wide receiver Randy Moss of the Minnesota Vikings and fearsome linebacker Junior Seau of the San Diego Chargers.

All eight players have overcome tough obstacles along the path to excellence and fame. It is their true grit, as well as their awesome talent, that make these players the greatest in the NFL. They are *8 of Today's Hottest NFL Stars!*

>> KURT WARNER

He went from supermarket to Super Bowl

Kurt Warner's story is so amazing that it is hard to believe that it is true. It reads more like a fairy tale.

In 1995, Kurt was working as a stock boy in a super-market in Iowa and dreaming of playing in the NFL. Five years later, he quarterbacked the St. Louis Rams to their first Super Bowl appearance. The story continues. . .

January 30, 2000: A crowd of 72,625 inside the Georgia Dome, in Atlanta, roars as the Rams and the Tennessee Titans lock horns in the final minutes of Super Bowl XXXIV. The Rams had led 16–0 as late as the middle of the third quarter, but the Titans have stormed back. With a little more than two minutes left in the fourth quarter, the Titans tie the score, 16–16, and are threatening to win the game.

When the Rams get the ball back, their offensive coach calls a pass play: "999 H–Balloon." Kurt drops back to pass and, with Titan defensive end Jevon Kearse bearing

down on him, he launches a bomb downfield. Wide receiver Isaac Bruce catches the ball on the Titan 43–yard line, jukes past two defenders, and races into the end zone. It's a 73–yard touchdown pass. The Rams take the lead.

Kurt never saw what happened. "I never really got a chance to see the catch," he said after the game. "I was down on the ground."

Kurt's touchdown pass was the winning margin as the Rams beat the Titans, 23–16, to become world champions. When the dust cleared, Kurt had passed for a Super Bowl record total of 414 yards and been named the game's Most Valuable Player (MVP).

With camera lights flashing and the Ram fans going absolutely bonkers, Kurt raised his arms in victory and looked into the crowd to find his wife, Brenda, who was also celebrating. It was a storybook ending to a fairy–tale season, one that proved that even the biggest dreams sometimes do come true.

A REAL-LIFE ROCKY

The fairy–tale season began during training camp in August 1999. Trent Green, the Rams' starting quarterback, suffered a knee injury. Kurt, the second–stringer, suddenly found himself the starter.

It was the break of a lifetime, and Kurt made the most of it. He threw 41 touchdown passes in the regular season to lead his Rams to a 13–3 record and earn regular–season NFL MVP honors. Then he added his playoff heroics.

"All I ever wanted was a chance," Kurt had told people before his surprising super season.

Kurt is, in many ways, a real–life football Rocky Balboa. Rocky is the boxer in the famous movie series. Rocky came out of nowhere to become world heavyweight boxing champion. Like Rocky, Kurt's life has been about overcoming huge challenges. Isaac Bruce told reporters that Kurt's story, "is better than Rocky, better than all the movies like that. This guy is real. He's lived it."

NO CAKEWALK

Kurt's early life was no cakewalk. He was born on June 22, 1971, in Burlington, Iowa. Kurt was four years old when his mom, Sue, and dad, Gene, divorced. Sue Warner needed three jobs to support the family after the divorce, but she always found time to give her kids love and discipline. When she was working, she made sure that Kurt and his older brother, Matt, kept in touch with her by phone.

Matt and Kurt were close. They shared a bedroom and a love of mischief. Kurt and Matt once took all the towels from the clothesline and gave them to neighborhood kids to use as capes so that they could play Batman and Superman.

Most of all, Kurt's mom taught her kids to chase their dreams, even though she thought that Kurt's fantasy about playing pro football was kind of far out.

Kurt wanted to be a wide receiver or defensive end, but unexpectedly, he wound up playing quarterback for Regis

High School. The kid trying out for quarterback was too small, so the coach asked Kurt if he could throw a football.

Kurt could throw, but he struggled to master the difficult position of quarterback. When the pressure was on and linemen were swarming down on him during a game, Kurt often ran instead of staying in the pocket and throwing.

His high school coaches created a special drill to keep him in the pocket. It was called "Kill Kurt." Two defensive linemen would whack Kurt with arm pads, then knock him down after he threw the ball. The idea was to get Kurt used to getting hit so that he would keep his wits about him and get the pass off. Kurt soon learned that, in game situations, anyway, the hits hurt a lot less when he completed the pass.

The punishing drills paid off. Kurt led Regis High to the state playoffs and a 7–2 record as a senior. He was chosen to play before college scouts in the Shrine Bowl, a game for top high school players from around the country.

A MOUNTAIN OF OBSTACLES

Kurt still had a mountain of obstacles to overcome to achieve his dream of playing pro football. He wanted to play at the University of Iowa, but the college had no interest in him. Neither did Iowa State. Kurt was offered a partial scholarship to Northern Iowa, a Division I–AA college. (Division I–A is the highest level of college sports;

Division I–AA is below that.) Even there, Kurt didn't start at quarterback until his senior year. When he did, he played well enough to be named the Gateway Conference's 1993 Offensive Player of the Year.

The Gateway Conference isn't well–known, so Kurt wasn't drafted by an NFL team. He was invited to the Green Bay Packers' training camp as a free agent in 1994, but he was cut. The Packers already had three standout quarterbacks: Brett Favre, Mark Brunell, and Ty Detmer. Kurt's dream of playing pro football took another big nosedive.

With nowhere to play, Kurt got a job stocking shelves at the Hy–Vee grocery store, in Cedar Falls, Iowa. He stayed in shape by working out during the day. He sometimes brought his football to the store at night and worked on his game by tossing passes down the aisle to his co–workers.

"I'll be playing football again someday," Kurt told them. His co–workers thought he was crazy. But Kurt kept going with the help of his strong belief in God, and in himself.

"I definitely felt I could play," Kurt said. "You have to believe in yourself even when nobody else does."

One day in 1995, Kurt got a call from the Iowa Barnstormers of the Arena Football League. Kurt was invited to try out for the team. He was almost cut, but he managed to hang on, and his pro career began — playing indoor football.

Arena football certainly wasn't the NFL. The teams travel on buses instead of planes, and play their games in small cities in basketball and hockey arenas. The quality of play isn't as good as in the NFL, either, but Kurt gained a lot from the experience. Playing on the small indoor fields (only 50 yards long, instead of 100, as in the NFL) taught him to read pass defenses quickly. He learned to throw into tight spots because there's less room for receivers to run on an indoor field. He developed a lightning–quick release and threw 183 touchdown passes in three seasons, from 1995 to 1997.

ADMIRAL WARNER

Kurt led Iowa to two straight Arena Bowl appearances. But it seemed he would never get a chance to play in the NFL. He was going to try out for the Chicago Bears, but he woke up one morning to find that the elbow of his throwing arm had swelled to the size of a baseball. A spider had bitten him. The Bears canceled the tryout.

Kurt later tried out for the Rams. They signed him, but that still didn't get him to the NFL. The Rams sent Kurt to play in Holland for the Amsterdam Admirals of NFL Europe, a pro league that develops players for NFL teams. Kurt played one season for Amsterdam, leading the league in passing and touchdowns.

Kurt's fine season overseas helped him get the third–string quarterback spot with the Rams in 1998. But he didn't get to play until the fourth quarter of the final game of the season. He completed four passes in 11 attempts, for 39 yards.

The Rams finished with a 4–12 record. The team did not look like future Super Bowl champions, nor did Kurt appear to be a world-beater.

KURT'S BIG BREAK

But things are not always as they seem. Kurt's big break was just around the corner. The Rams' starting quarterback, Trent Green, suffered a serious knee injury in a preseason game against the San Diego Chargers on August 28, 1999. The Rams' first regular-season game was only two weeks away, so head coach Dick Vermeil turned to Kurt.

"I thought he would be a guy we could get by with," Coach Vermeil told *Sports Illustrated.* "I didn't expect him to play well enough that we'd win because of him."

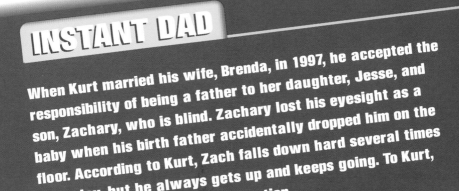

INSTANT DAD

When Kurt married his wife, Brenda, in 1997, he accepted the responsibility of being a father to her daughter, Jesse, and son, Zachary, who is blind. Zachary lost his eyesight as a baby when his birth father accidentally dropped him on the floor. According to Kurt, Zach falls down hard several times each day, but he always gets up and keeps going. To Kurt, Zach is a blessing and an inspiration.

Kurt got off to a hot start. He threw 14 TD passes in his first four games. The Rams won all four. Against the San Francisco 49ers on October 10, Kurt threw for 177 yards and three TDs in the first quarter. His final stats that day were 20 completions in 23 attempts for 323 yards and five TDs.

As the Rams kept winning, Kurt began to receive a lot of attention from the media. He had to change his home phone number because of all the requests for interviews. But Kurt stayed humble and focused. "Kurt's the most grounded person you'll ever meet," said then Ram cornerback Todd Lyght. "There's no way he'll let this go to his head."

Kurt stayed calm through the playoffs. After the Rams beat the Minnesota Vikings, 49–37, in the divisional game, Kurt celebrated by going home. "I ate pizza and hung out with my family," he says. "I watched a movie with my daughter."

The Rams' next opponent was the tough Tampa Bay Buccaneers, in the NFC Championship Game. The Rams were trailing, 6–5, with about five minutes left in the game when Kurt zipped a 30-yard pass to wideout Ricky Proehl for a touchdown. The Rams won, 11–6.

Before the Super Bowl, Kurt told reporters: "I've learned a lot along the way about perseverance, being humble, and enjoying everything you've got."

Then he went out and enjoyed the biggest game of his life.

SUPER BOWL REPEATERS?

Kurt and the Rams looked to repeat as NFL champs in 2000. On the strength of Kurt's right arm, St. Louis won its first six games. Kurt passed for at least 300 yards in each win. He threw four touchdowns in two different games and 18 touchdowns in the six-game stretch.

In the Rams' seventh game of the season, Kurt broke a finger on his throwing hand. The injury kept him out of action for the next five games. During that time, the Rams went only 2–3. Kurt returned for the last four games of the regular season, but in the last game of the season, against the New Orleans Saints, Kurt suffered a concussion. He returned to play in the Rams' opening-round playoff game against the Saints and tossed for a game-high 365 yards. But the Rams lost, 31–28, and their dream of a repeat championship was over. On the season, Kurt threw for 3,429 yards on 235 completions. He had 21 touchdown passes.

With the off-season to fully recover from his aches and pains, Kurt eyed another Super Bowl title in 2001. He came out firing, leading the Rams to an NFL-best 14–2 record. Kurt passed for over 300 yards in a game nine times and even had a 401-yard performance against the New England Patriots in a 24–17 victory. In three different games, he burned the opposition with four touchdown passes.

Kurt was the top-rated quarterback in the league, leading all passers in completions (375), yards (4,830), and touchdowns (36). For his stellar performance, Kurt was once again awarded the league MVP award.

In the playoffs, the Rams beat the Green Bay Packers, 45–17, in the opening-round divisional playoff game. Kurt passed for 216 yards and two touchdowns. The Rams then edged

KURT KIBBLES

Birth Date June 22, 1971

Height 6 feet 2 inches

Weight 220 lbs.

Home Johnston, Iowa

College Degree Communications

Breakfast Bowl A cereal is named after Kurt: Warner's Crunch Time. Money from the sale of the cereal is given to camps for kids in Missouri who need special physical and emotional care.

the Philadelphia Eagles in the conference championship game, 29–24. Kurt had another fine afternoon, hitting on 22 of 33 attempts for 212 yards and one touchdown. The win set the stage for another Ram Super Bowl appearance.

On February 3, 2002, St. Louis went up against the New England Patriots in Super Bowl XXXVI, in New Orleans, Louisiana. In a stunning upset victory, the Pats beat St. Louis, 20–17, on a fourth quarter field goal by Adam Vinatieri with no time left on the clock. Kurt had rallied the Rams in the final quarter with two touchdown drives to tie the game, 17-17. Playing with an injured right thumb, Kurt completed 28 of 44 passes for 365 yards and one TD. Still, it was a disappointing end to a terrific season.

But Kurt has always believed that, "as long as you keep that dream alive inside of you, anything is possible." To his family, teammates, fans, and all the dreamers of the world, Kurt is a hero and an inspiration. He's a man who dared to dream an impossible dream, and then he made it happen.

He's a real-life Rocky.

>> RANDY MOSS

This dazzling receiver almost fumbled his life and career

Randy Moss, the Minnesota Vikings' awesome wide receiver, is called "Super Freak." He has a needle-thin 6-foot-4-inch body and big, soft hands. He's faster than a jackrabbit with its tail on fire, and he can leap more than three feet into the air. Quarterbacks love passing to Randy because they can throw the ball about 12 feet high, and he will jump and stretch like a Slinky to grab it.

"I try to catch everything," says Randy. "If the ball is in the air, I want it."

Randy played only two seasons in the NFL before people started comparing him with such all-time great receivers as Jerry Rice of the San Francisco 49ers, Art Monk of the Washington Redskins, and Lynn Swann of the Pittsburgh Steelers. In 1998, Randy was the NFL Rookie of the Year. He followed that sparkling season by leading the NFC in receiving yards (1,413) in 1999.

There's no telling how good Randy can become. He became so good so quickly, it's scary. What is even scarier is the way he almost let his life — and his football career — slip through his fingers.

EARLY TROUBLES

Randy was born on February 13, 1977, in Rand, West Virginia. His dad left home before Randy was born. His mom, Maxine, was a nurse's aide who worked two jobs to support her three kids.

Randy was a terrific, all-around athlete at DuPont High School, in Rand. He played point guard and was twice selected as West Virginia's Mr. Basketball. He played centerfield for the baseball team and attracted the attention of major league scouts. He also won state and conference championships as a sprinter on the track team. And none of those was even his best sport.

Football was Randy's best sport. Head coach Lou Holtz of the University of Notre Dame called Randy the best high school player he had ever seen. Coach Holtz offered Randy a scholarship. Randy fumbled that opportunity by beating up a classmate whom Randy thought had carved a racial insult on a desk at DuPont High School. Randy was sentenced to 30 days in jail. Notre Dame canceled his scholarship.

Coach Holtz recommended Randy to Bobby Bowden, the head coach at Florida State University (FSU). Coach Bowden watched Randy turn defenders inside-out in practice and said, "He has greatness written all over him."

Randy attended FSU but didn't play as a freshman because Coach Bowden wanted to give him time to get used to living away from home. Randy never got the chance to play for FSU as a sophomore because he failed a drug test given by the school. The test showed that Randy had smoked marijuana. A judge sent him back to jail for 60 days. Florida State canceled Randy's scholarship.

With two strikes against him, Randy enrolled at Marshall University, in Huntington, West Virginia, and joined the football team. He had a lot to prove.

Randy proved how talented he was as a football player by tying Jerry Rice's single-season college record of 28 TD catches. He also led Marshall to the 1996 Southern Conference Championship and the Division I-AA championship.

But the day after the Marshall football team clinched the Southern Conference championship, police arrested Randy and his girlfriend for fighting with each other. The charges were later dropped, but the damage had been done. The word got out that Randy was nothing but a troublemaker. He caught 90 passes for 25 touchdowns as a sophomore, and decided to leave college and enter the 1998 NFL draft. He soon discovered that most teams were afraid to draft him. It no longer seemed to matter that Randy was the best wide receiver in the draft. Except to the Minnesota Vikings, that is.

BETTER LATE...

Randy is just one of many superstars who were chosen later in the NFL draft than you might expect. Wide receiver Jerry Rice of the 49ers was the 16th pick, in 1985. Quarterback Brett Favre of the Packers was the 33rd pick (by the Atlanta Falcons), in 1991. Defensive end Michael Strahan of the Giants was the 40th pick, in 1993. And our "latest" champ: Running back Terrell Davis of the Broncos was the 196th pick, in 1995.

NOT A BAD GUY

Viking scouts talked to people who knew Randy well, including his half–brother Eric, who was an offensive lineman on the Vikings. "We did our homework," says Frank Gilliam, the team's vice president in charge of players. "Many of his problems happened when he was very young. We're not going to defend it, but we listened to people who knew him. His brother said that Randy had made mistakes, but that he wasn't a bad guy."

Viking head coach Dennis Green believed Randy would be fine because he would be surrounded by his brother and level–headed teammates, such as All–Pro wide receiver Cris Carter.

"I knew what we were bringing Randy into," Coach Green told *Sports Illustrated.* "My players know what is expected, and they will take care of things long before I know about it."

Randy really wanted to play for the Dallas Cowboys, but they chose another player, as did 20 other teams. The Cincinnati Bengals had two first-round picks but twice decided against taking him. The Vikings finally made Randy the 21st player chosen in the draft.

THE PUPIL AND THE MASTER

Cris Carter soon took Randy under his wing. Randy looked up to Cris because Cris had survived hard times. Using booze and drugs had cost Cris his first job, with the Philadelphia Eagles, and taught him a tough lesson. Cris quit drugs and alcohol and put his life back on track.

Cris let Randy stay with him at his home in Florida. They worked out together, and Cris gave the rookie some advice: "I told him there are no excuses. He has been given a tremendous opportunity to mature and handle his life. You have to experience things to grow up, and he will."

Randy brought a truckload of confidence to training camp that summer. With diamond studs in his ears and tattoos on his chest and arms, he was a picture of cockiness. The Viking coaches told him that he would be the third wide receiver. Cris Carter and Jake Reed would start. Randy would join them for about half the plays.

Randy didn't seem to mind. He helped make the Vikings the NFL's most exciting team that season. Their "PlayStation Offense" rang up big scores like a video game, smashing the NFL single-season record for most points by one team (556).

Randy's coming-out party was a Monday night game in October against the Green Bay Packers. The game was seen on national television. Viking quarterback Randall Cunningham walked over to Randy's locker before the game and asked, "Are you scared?"

Randy gave Randall a funny look and replied, "What do you mean, scared?"

"Don't you know it's Monday night?" Randall asked. "All those people out there, everybody watching?"

Randy just stared back and said, "Hey, let's get it on."

Randy went out and hauled in five passes for 190 yards. Two of his catches were spectacular touchdowns of 52 and 44 yards. He caught passes for big gains of 41 and 46 yards. He also had a 75-yard TD catch, but it didn't count because the Vikings were penalized for holding during the play. The Vikings won, 37–24.

The game made Randy a national star. Waves of reporters interviewed him after the game.

"I don't care if we play on TV, how big the crowd is, I just want to play," he told them. "I feel very blessed to be here."

Randall Cunningham added, "I feel blessed to have Randy on this team. You throw it up there and he'll get it. He's fun to watch."

LIGHTING IT UP

Randy caught 69 passes, for 1,313 yards, that season. He led the NFL in TD catches (17), a rookie record, and was chosen for the Pro Bowl. The Vikings finished 15–1, but lost the NFC Championship Game to the Atlanta Falcons, 30–27, in overtime. Randy's great season made him say cocky things such as, "I don't think the NFL is cracked up to what it's supposed to be. I expected more."

Some people expected more from Randy.

Former All-Pro receiver Ozzie Newsome told the *Sporting News*: "Let's give him three years to see if he learns to respect the league and has the mental maturity to become great. By then, we'll all know he has handled stuff both off and on the field."

MOSS MORSELS

Birth Date February 13, 1977

Height 6 feet 4 inches

Weight 198 lbs.

Home Boca Raton, Florida

Fast Fact Guard Jason Williams of the Memphis Grizzlies was Randy's high school basketball teammate

Hobbies Fishing, swimming, and basketball

Secret Talent He can play the drums

Randy caught 80 passes, for 1,413 yards, in 1999, but the St. Louis Rams beat the Vikings, 49–37, in the playoffs. Randy snagged nine passes for 188 yards and two TDs against the Rams, but he stained his reputation by angrily squirting a water bottle at a referee in the fourth quarter. The NFL fined Randy $40,000, and he was widely criticized by fans, sportswriters, and broadcasters.

Was Randy still an immature punk? He didn't think so.

As for his past, Randy says, "I don't think about it. It's gone, it's over, and I've learned from it. I'm just looking forward to the future."

BEST SEASON AS A PRO

Randy's 2000 season was his best as a pro. He caught 77 passes for 1,437 yards. His 16 TD receptions led all NFL receivers. No receiver in NFL history had better stats in his first three seasons in the league than Randy.

The Vikings rolled to an 11–5 record, tops in the NFC Central Division. The Vikes beat the New Orleans Saints, 34–16, in the opening round of the playoffs. But Minnesota was badly beaten by the New York Giants in the NFC title game, 41–0. Randy suffered a severely bruised rib in the game and was held to only two receptions for 18 yards.

During the season, Randy had gotten into trouble again. He was fined $40,000 in October of 2000 for making contact with an official during a game. Randy felt the heat from league officials, fans, and reporters. Once again, people started to question Randy's ability to stay out of trouble.

MORE UPS AND DOWNS

In the 2001 season, the Vikings sank to a 5–11 record, going a dismal 0–8 in road games. Randy had his share of fine moments, notching four games in which he caught passes for 140 yards or more. His best game of the season came against the New York Giants on November 18. In a 28–16 Viking win, Randy snared 10 passes for a season-high 171 yards and three touchdowns.

Randy had a personal–best 82 receptions on the season, for 1,233 yards. But his 10 touchdown receptions were the fewest in a single season in his career.

Trouble found Randy several times in the 2001 season. In December, he was fined $15,000 for verbally abusing a group of corporate sponsors on a team bus. (The Vikings, like most NFL teams, often invite top executives of the companies that advertise with them to road games.) The *Twin Cities Star Tribune* reported that Randy got upset to find the seat he wanted being used by a sponsor.

The bus incident was Randy's third fine of the season. Earlier, he had been fined $20,000 by the NFL — twice for taunting and once for wearing an unapproved cap on the sideline during a pre–season game.

People are hoping that Randy can keep his emotions in check and concentrate on playing the high–caliber brand of football of which he's capable. They know he's got a bright future and is surely on a straight path to the NFL Hall of Fame . . . if he keeps his nose clean.

>> DREW BLEDSOE

The Patriots' quarterback is the NFL's king of comebacks

Don't ever count out the New England Patriots when quarterback Drew Bledsoe is in the game. Too many teams have started to celebrate what seemed like a certain victory over the Patriots, only to be stunned by Drew's heroics in the final seconds.

Drew is a magician. But instead of pulling a rabbit out of a hat, he pulls victory out of the jaws of defeat. During his first seven seasons in the NFL, Drew led the Patriots to 15 dramatic comeback wins. As the clock ticks down and the pressure rises, most people start to get very nervous. Not Drew. He stays as cool as a cucumber and works his magic.

NEVER TOO LATE

Things looked bleak for the Patriots in a September 1999 home game against the Indianapolis Colts. The Pats trailed, 28–7, late in third quarter. But Drew was just

getting started. He led his team 81 yards in 10 plays. The last play was a sharp, eight-yard touchdown pass to running back Terry Allen that made the score 28–14.

Several minutes later, the Patriots recovered a Colt fumble near midfield. Drew led another drive, capping it off with a three-yard touchdown pass to tight end Ben Coates. The score: Colts 28, Patriots 21.

The next time the Patriots got the ball, Drew led them on a 78-yard march. He hooked up with Ben for a game-tying, 10-yard TD toss. There were 3 minutes 3 seconds left in the game.

The Colts were shaking in their cleats. They fumbled the ball on their own 37-yard line with 2 minutes 37 seconds left to play. The Pats recovered the ball, and Drew drove them toward the goal line again. With 35 seconds left, Adam Vinatieri kicked a 26-yard field goal. Final score: Patriots 31, Colts 28.

"The only way we were going to be out of that game was if we panicked, and we didn't panic," Drew told reporters. "We can come back in any game, and we showed that today."

BECOMING MR. COOL

"One of my strengths as a quarterback is I'm able to stay calm when it's chaotic," Drew told the *Providence Journal-Bulletin* after the Patriots' comeback win against the Colts.

Drew worked to develop that ability. As a teenager, he admired Denver Bronco quarterback John Elway, the NFL's king of comebacks in those days. John was at his best when a game was on the line and time was running out. He led the Broncos to 35 fourth-quarter comebacks during his 16 NFL seasons.

Drew was born on February 14, 1972, in Ellensburg, Washington, and grew up in the small city of Walla Walla. He was the oldest of Mac and Barbara Bledsoe's two boys.

Drew's dad was an assistant football coach at Walla Walla High School. Drew grew up with the game. "It was nice to sit around the dinner table and talk about football," he told the *New York Daily News*. "I learned football like a lot of kids learned language. A lot of things I see and react to on the field seem like common sense to me."

Drew began playing quarterback for his school team in eighth grade. He attended summer football camps, where he learned about directing a last-minute touchdown drive. "How to manage the clock, which play to call. It's always been my favorite time of the game, the time I feel most comfortable," Drew told the *Providence Journal-Bulletin*.

By the time he entered Walla Walla High School, in 1986, Drew was motivated to succeed. He carried little notes in his pockets. The notes said things like I HUSTLE ON EVERY PLAY and I'M THE FIRST ON THE FIELD AND THE LAST TO LEAVE. He took his notes to heart and won all-state honors.

BLIZZARD OF AHHS

Drew attended Washington State University, where he became the first freshman in 30 years to start at quarterback for the school. As a junior, in 1992, he showed he had a knack for overcoming obstacles when he led his team to victory in a blizzard. Eight inches of snow fell during the game, but Drew threw for 260 yards and two touchdowns. Washington State beat Washington, 42–23.

Drew capped off his junior season by setting a school passing record. He threw for 476 yards against the University of Utah in the Copper Bowl, a post-season game played in Tucson, Arizona. He felt ready to take on pro defenses and entered the NFL draft after that season. The Patriots made him the first player chosen in the 1993 draft.

The Patriots were an awful team that had a 2–14 record in 1992. Drew was expected to make them winners. The pressure was on. The team's head coach was the fiery Bill Parcells. He stood behind Drew in practice and yelled, "You stink!" if Drew messed up. Drew got angry, but he kept quiet. He knew his coach was trying to make him tough enough to handle intense pressure and criticism.

Drew struggled as the Pats lost 11 of their first 12 games in 1993. He hit bottom against the Steelers on December 5, when he fumbled four times and threw five interceptions. "That game was one of the best things that could have happened to me," Drew told *Sports Illustrated*. "Suddenly, I realized I might be a bust. That's pretty humbling."

Drew buckled down and tried even harder. The Patriots finished strong by winning their last four games. His breakthrough came the next season, 1994. He led the NFL in completions (400) and passing yards (4,555). That season's highlight was the miracle comeback he led in a November

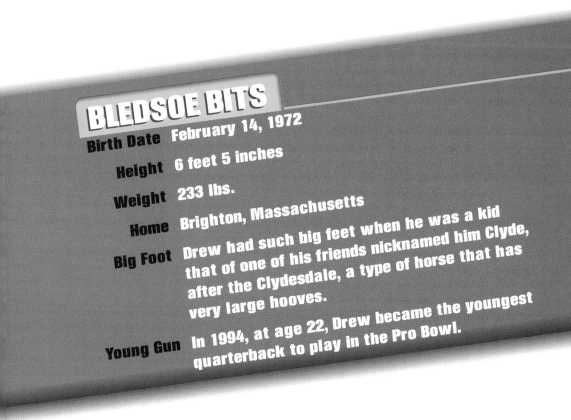

BLEDSOE BITS

Birth Date February 14, 1972

Height 6 feet 5 inches

Weight 233 lbs.

Home Brighton, Massachusetts

Big Foot Drew had such big feet when he was a kid that of one of his friends nicknamed him Clyde, after the Clydesdale, a type of horse that has very large hooves.

Young Gun In 1994, at age 22, Drew became the youngest quarterback to play in the Pro Bowl.

game against the Vikings. The Pats were down 20–3 when Drew threw a TD pass on the opening drive of the third quarter to make the score 20–10. Then, with only 2 minutes 27 seconds left in the game, he threw a TD to make the score 20–17.

When the Patriots got the ball again, they had time for one last drive. When the Vikings seemed to have stopped them, the Patriots were left in a tough situation: They had the ball on their own 39-yard line, and it was fourth down with 10 yards to go for a first down. Then Mr. Cool showed his stuff! With 1 minute 51 seconds left to play in the game, Drew completed a 25-yard pass to Vincent Brisby. He completed his next four passes to reach the Viking five-yard line, and Patriot placekicker Matt Bahr kicked the game-tying field goal.

In overtime, the Patriots got the ball on their 33-yard line and started driving. Drew completed five passes to bring his team to the Viking 25. Three more plays gained 11 yards. The Patriots lined up again. Across the line of scrimmage, Viking defensive tackle John Randle shook his finger at Drew, as if to say "You're going down, kid!" Drew waved back, as if to say, "Come and get me!"

Drew took the snap and lobbed the ball to running back Kevin Turner, who had darted into a corner of the end zone. *Touchdown!* The Pats won, 26–20. What a comeback.

In the locker room, Coach Parcells was so proud of Drew that he could barely talk. "You've given me hope," said Coach Parcells, choking up. "That was valiant."

After that miracle comeback against the Vikings, the Pats went on a seven-game winning streak. They reached the playoffs for the first time in eight seasons. They lost to the Cleveland Browns, 20–13, in the AFC wild-card game, but still, they had taken a big step in the right direction.

The Pats struggled in 1995, finishing 6–10. They bounced back to go 11–5 in 1996, winning their division and reaching the Super Bowl, their first in 11 seasons. Drew was only 24 years old! The Pats lost to Green Bay, 35–21. But Drew became one of the NFL's biggest stars.

STILL THE ONE

In the seasons that followed, Drew continued to make his mark in the NFL. Drew led the Pats to a 10–6 record in 1997, as they won their division for the second straight season — for the first time in franchise history. The Pats defeated the Miami Dolphins, 17–13, in a wild–card playoff game, but lost to the Pittsburgh Steelers, 7–6, in the division playoff game. Drew passed for a career–high 28 touchdowns in 1997.

New England went 9–7 in 1998, making the playoffs for the third consecutive season — another team record that Drew had engineered. However, they lost to the Jacksonville Jaguars, 25–10, in the wild–card game. Drew had another big year in 1999, throwing for 3,985 yards — only 15 yards short of what would have been his second 4,000–plus yard seasons. The Pats finished 8–8.

Drew suffered a badly bruised thumb in the middle of the 2000 season, but he continued his run at the record books. He became the Patriots' all–time leading passer, breaking Steve Grogan's record of 26,886 career passing yards. Drew also became only the fourth quarterback in NFL history to have seven consecutive 3,000–plus passing yard seasons. He joined Dan Marino, Brett Favre, and John Elway as the others who accomplished the feat. Unfortunately, the Pats finished the season with an 8–8 record, failing to make the playoffs.

One of New England's biggest problems in 2000 was its inability to protect its quarterback. Drew spent most of the season running for his life, trying to avoid defensive opponents. He spent lots of time on his back, as the Pats allowed 48 sacks. (In his first *three* seasons — 48 games — Drew was sacked only 61 times.)

A NEW DEAL

Before the start of the 2001 season, Drew signed a 10-year $103 million contract with New England. It was the biggest contract in NFL history and almost assured that Drew would be with the Pats until the day he retired. "I've expressed over and over again my desire to play my entire career with the New England Patriots. It looks like that is a very real possibility," Drew said after signing.

But the future of Drew's career came into doubt in the Pats' second game of the 2001 season. In a game against the New York Jets, Drew was hit at full-speed by linebacker Mo Lewis. Drew played in one more series of downs before he was taken out of the game. He was rushed to the hospital right after the Patriots' loss. Doctors determined that Drew had internal bleeding in his chest cavity. This was serious business.

The injury dropped the curtain on Drew's season. Second-year pro Tom Brady became the Pats' starting quarterback. Tom had never started an NFL game and had thrown only three passes in his NFL career. But he filled in extremely well. In the meantime, Drew had recuperated and was available for action by the Pats' 11th game of the season.

But New England head coach Bill Belichick stayed with Tom as his regular quarterback. Tom guided the Pats to an

11–5 record, winning the last seven games of the regular season. Drew patiently watched from the sidelines as the Pats headed into the playoffs.

New England topped the Oakland Raiders in the divisional playoff game and then took on the Pittsburgh Steelers for the conference title. That's when the nearly forgotten Drew Bledsoe reminded everyone why he's one of the NFL's best players.

While completing a 28–yard pass late in the second quarter, Tom was hit by Steeler safety Lee Flowers. Tom's leg was injured on the play and he was forced to leave the game.

Enter Drew Bledsoe.

With another trip to the Super Bowl on the line, Drew took control and calmly began to pick apart the Steelers' defense. The big play was an 11–yard touchdown pass to David Patten. Drew guided the Pats to another touchdown and a field goal in the second half. The Pats won the game, 24–17, and earned a shot at the NFL championship. On the day, Drew completed 10 of 21 passes for 102 yards and a touchdown. His cool–headed leadership was the key to New England's stunning upset win.

"You don't give a guy $103 million if you don't think he can be a championship quarterback," said Steeler Lee Flowers. "He's a good quarterback. No one on our sidelines was celebrating when Brady went out."

Drew humbly downplayed his amazing performance. "I've been at this for a long time and at times at a pretty high level. I felt confident coming out. I've been working hard and preparing for this exact scenario," he said after the victory.

In the week leading up to the Super Bowl, Coach Belichick had a tough decision to make: Who would he choose to be his starting quarterback in Super Bowl XXXVI against the St. Louis Rams? Coach Belichick decided to go with Tom. Drew handled Coach Belichick's decision by putting the good of the team ahead of his personal feelings.

"Obviously, it's a disappointing situation," Drew said. "Everybody would love to be playing in this game. I'm just going to do whatever I can to to help Tom and help prepare myself and be ready to play if that opportunity comes up."

Drew didn't see any action in what was one of the most exciting Super Bowls in many years. The Patriots came out on top with a thrilling 20–17 victory. With the game tied at 17–17, New England kicker Adam Vinatieri booted a fourth-quarter, 48–yard field goal with no time remaining on the clock. The Pats had won their first NFL championship.

THE PRANKSTER

Drew is all business in a game, but off the field he loves pulling practical jokes on his teammates. After being the target of his pranks, a couple of his teammates got even. Drew once went to the players' parking lot to get his truck. All he found was a big pile of snow where his truck used to be. At first, Drew couldn't figure it out. Then he realized his teammates had buried his truck under the snow.

Drew spent several hours digging out his truck, but he didn't get mad. He got his prankster mind working again. When he later heard that one of the jokers was guard Todd Rucci, Drew hired a moving company and told them what to do. When Todd came home from practice one day, his home was empty. The movers had put all of Todd's furniture in the basement!

On the field, Drew does the moving, and he's serious about it. When Mr. Cool is moving the Patriots down the field on one of his come–from–behind drives, opponents watch out. They know that he could start weaving his magic at any moment. And that's no joke.

NEWSFLASH!

On April 21, 2002, Drew was traded by the Patriots to the Buffalo Bills. Drew is excited to be a team's number one quarterback once again. "I think it's going to be a very, very positive change for me. And hopefully a positive change for the Buffalo Bills," Drew said.

>> STEVE McNAIR

"Air McNair" is the NFL's most electrifying quarterback

At 6 feet 2 inches and a rock–solid 225 pounds, Steve McNair looks more like a running back than the quarterback that he is. The Tennessee Titan star sometimes even *plays* more like a running back. He carries the ball and zooms around tacklers or bowls them over like a runaway locomotive.

Steve is also an excellent passer. What a combination. His powerhouse running and deadly passing have made him one of the most menacing double threats in the NFL.

Steve gave the St. Louis Rams all they could handle in the second half of Super Bowl XXXIV, in January 2000. Trailing 16–0 in the third quarter, Steve led the Titans to a pair of touchdowns and the field goal that tied the game with two minutes 12 seconds left to play. It was one of the greatest rallies in Super Bowl history.

The Rams quickly replied with a touchdown to take a 23–16 lead, but Steve fearlessly led the Titans on a heart-stopping 87-yard drive as the game's final seconds

ticked away. He rushed, scrambled, ducked under and between defenders, and threw bullet passes as the Titans marched toward the Ram goal line.

With 22 seconds left and the ball on the Ram 26-yard line, Steve scrambled as two Ram defenders chased him. Just when it seemed certain that Steve would be snowed under, he somehow slipped out of the grasp of both Rams and threw a desperate pass to wideout Kevin Dyson. Kevin caught the ball and was tackled at the 10-yard line. The Titans called their final timeout. The crowd held its breath.

Six seconds were left on the clock. The Titans needed 10 yards to tie the score and send the game into overtime. On this final drive, Steve had completed six passes for 48 yards and run twice for 14 more to set a Super Bowl record for rushing yards by a quarterback in one game (64).

Steve called the pass play "Sliver Right" in the huddle. When he took the snap, he dropped back and fired a quick slant over the middle to Kevin. But Kevin had cut toward the middle of the field too quickly. Ram linebacker Mike Jones brought Kevin down one yard short of the goal line as time ran out. The Rams had held on to win, 23–16.

It was a super-tough defeat for Steve, but he held his head high. "We just came up short," he told reporters after the game. "We were able to get some Super Bowl experience. When we come back next time, we'll feel more comfortable. We're only going to get better."

That's a scary thought if you have to play against Steve.

A SPECIAL DISTINCTION

In January 2000, Steve earned a special place in NFL history when he became only the second black quarterback to start in a Super Bowl. Doug Williams was the first to do it. Doug led the Washington Redskins to a 42-10 victory over the Denver Broncos in Super Bowl XXII. The game was played in 1988.

NO FEAR

Steve has no fear of tough challenges. He got his fierce determination to succeed from his mom. Lucille McNair was a take-charge mother who encouraged her son to be a take-charge young man. Mrs. McNair told reporters at the Super Bowl: "Steve is like me. He never complains. He knows how to work for what he wants and how to earn it."

Steve learned those lessons growing up in the country town of Mount Olive, Mississippi. He was born on February 14, 1973, and shared a small, three-bedroom house with his mom and his four brothers.

Mrs. McNair was the strict head of her household. She had been raised in a disciplined house by a single mom who had 11 kids. When she and her husband separated,

Steve's mom became a single mom too. Mrs. McNair worked long hours for many years to raise her sons on her own. She worked overnight at a factory and struggled to pay the bills while keeping her growing boys fed and clothed. Steve's younger brother, Michael, was born when Steve was 14. But when Steve was growing up, he was the youngest kid. His three older brothers, Fred, Tim, and Jason, pitched in to help care for him.

McNAIR TIDBITS

Birth Date February 14, 1973

Height 6 feet 2 inches

Weight 225 lbs.

Home Mount Olive, Mississippi

Nickname Monk (short for Monkey). Steve's mom gave him the nickname when he was a kid because he liked to climb and swing in a tree near his home.

Young Gun After he signed his first pro contract in 1995, Steve built a home for his mom. When he took her to the land where the house was to be built, she started to cry. It was the place where she had picked cotton as a girl. Steve didn't know that when he bought the land.

The McNair boys loved to play football for hours each day, near a cow pasture. Steve pretended to be Terry Bradshaw, the great quarterback who had led the Pittsburgh Steelers to four Super Bowl victories from 1975 to 1980.

Steve dreamed of being a pro quarterback, but few black quarterbacks had played in the NFL, so he was facing a stiff challenge. Blacks usually played running back, receiver, or defensive positions in college and the NFL. People suspected that many coaches and scouts didn't think blacks were good enough to play quarterback. Few black players even got a chance to show what they could do at the position.

At Mount Olive High, Steve was an all-state selection at quarterback and defensive back. He also excelled at basketball and baseball. But during his senior year, he found out that no major colleges were interested in him as a quarterback. "The big schools only wanted me to play defense," Steve said. "I don't want to say it was because I'm black. But you wonder what they're thinking."

WORKING HIS WAY UP

If Steve wanted to play quarterback, he would have to do it at a small college. Before he made his decision, Steve thought about quitting football. He had been offered a contract by the Seattle Mariners to play pro baseball. He wondered if the same thing would happen to him that happened to his older brother, Fred, who was a top college quarterback during his senior season. Fred wasn't drafted by an NFL team. He ended up playing for the Florida Bobcats of the indoor Arena Football League.

But Steve didn't give up. He decided to attend little Alcorn State University, in Mississippi. He was dead-set on making himself into a quarterback that NFL scouts would notice.

"I don't want to give them any reason to doubt me," Steve told reporters. "I want to have a quick release like Dan Marino. I want to read defenses like Joe Montana. I want to throw the deep ball like Drew Bledsoe. I want to throw on the run like Randall Cunningham." (Joe, Dan, Drew, and Randall were all outstanding NFL quarterbacks at the time.)

AIR McNAIR

At Alcorn State, Steve threw bombs and quick strikes. He set the national college record for total offense with 16,823 total yards of rushing and passing during his four years there. As a senior, he finished third in the voting for the 1994 Heisman Trophy, which is awarded to the best player in college football. He attracted NFL scouts like bees to honey. The Houston Oilers chose him third overall in the 1995 NFL draft. Steve was the first quarterback chosen in the draft.

Steve's first two NFL seasons were hard. He spent most of his first season on the inactive list, as the third-string quarterback. The next season, he was a backup to Chris Chandler and played in only four games. When Chris was traded, in 1997, Steve got a chance to become the starter.

He passed for 2,665 yards and led the team in rushing touchdowns with eight. But the Oilers finished 8–8 that season.

They hadn't made the playoffs since the 1993 season. Some people doubted that Steve was good enough to make the Oilers a winning team again.

Oiler head coach Jeff Fisher believed that Steve *was* just the guy to turn the team around.

"If you were going to put together a list of all the things you can't teach — poise, ability to lead, competitiveness, responsibility — Steve has them all," Coach Fisher told *Sports Illustrated.*

The Oilers finished 8–8 again in 1998, even though Steve became the youngest quarterback in the team's 38-year history to pass for 3,000 yards or more. He also led all NFL quarterbacks in rushing for the second season in a row.

The Oilers had been having a tough time playing without a true home stadium, and true home fans, for two seasons. Before the 1997 season, the Oilers moved from Houston, Texas, to Memphis, Tennessee, where they played one season at the Liberty Bowl. Then they moved to Nashville, Tennessee, for 1998. That season, they played in Vanderbilt Stadium while their new stadium was built.

Everything finally settled down in 1999. The Oilers had flashy new blue uniforms, a new name — the Tennessee Titans — and a new stadium: Adelphia Coliseum. Steve missed five regular-season games with a back injury but returned to the lineup for good on October 31.

Steve passed for 2,179 yards, led NFL quarterbacks in rushing (337 yards), and threw only eight interceptions.

The Titans roared into the playoffs with a 13–3 record, became AFC champions, then made their dramatic run in the Super Bowl against the Rams.

FALLING SHORT

If the Titans thought that anything could hurt as much as their disappointing Super Bowl loss, they didn't know what was in store for them in 2000. After posting another 13–3 league-leading record, the Titans had good reason to eye another shot at the NFL title. But it wasn't to be. The Baltimore Ravens slammed the door on the Titans' championship hopes with a 24–10 victory in the division title game.

Although Steve completed 24 passes, he was unable to throw any touchdowns and was intercepted once. The Titans old weakness of settling for field goal attempts instead of touchdowns hurt them badly in their loss to the Ravens: three Titan drives ended with failed field goal attempts by kicker Al Del Greco.

Steve recognized the Titans' failings in the big game. "In order for us to be a dominant team in the NFL, we have to score at will and be consistent. With a little incentive, that'll help us get better for next year," Steve said.

Despite the loss, Steve had had another fine showing in the 2000 season, establishing a career-best passing percentage of 62.6. He had 248 completions, 2,847 yards, and 17 touchdowns.

THE BIG HURT

Three days after the loss to Baltimore, Steve started feeling pain in his right shoulder. The pain kept him out of his first Pro Bowl appearance. Steve was afraid that the pain might end his NFL career, or worse — prevent him from ever lifting his arm above his head again. In February 2001, Steve had surgery on the shoulder. It brought immediate relief. A thankful Steve said, "I was really scared. The pain was like no other. It was just constantly aching."

With a healthy quarterback calling signals in the 2001 season, the Titans were planning on another winning season. Tennessee was among the favorite teams to make a Super Bowl appearance. Instead, they finished with a poor 7–9 record — their first below -.500 season since 1995.

But Steve passed for a career-high 21 touchdowns to go along with a 61.3 percent pass completion rate and 3,350 yards. He ran for another 414 yards and scored five TDs on the ground.

The Titans have had plenty of ups and downs in the last few seasons, but Steve has proved beyond all doubt that he is one of the NFL's most talented — and exciting — quarterbacks.

JUNIOR SEAU

The NFL's most ferocious linebacker is never satisfied

The San Diego Chargers were leading the Kansas City Chiefs, 14–3, in the second quarter of a 1999 pre-season game. The Chargers had the ball on Kansas City's 37-yard line when all-pro linebacker Junior Seau [*SAY-ow*] trotted off the Charger bench and joined the huddle.

It's unusual for a linebacker to play when his team has the ball, but Junior is an unusual linebacker. When the ball was snapped, Junior raced down the left sideline. He was wide open when Charger quarterback Jim Harbaugh zipped the ball to him for a 37-yard touchdown.

A NEW THREAT

Junior is best known as the ball-seeking missile of the Charger defense. If you have the ball, Junior will zero in on you and — *wham, bam!* That hurts! Junior is 6 feet 3 inches tall and weighs 250 pounds. He has made more than 1,200 bone-crunching tackles during his 12 NFL seasons. He played in his 11th straight Pro Bowl in February 2002!

THE JUNIOR PACKAGE

In training camp before the 1999 season, Junior told Charger coach Mike Riley that he wanted to contribute to the team on offense. The Charger coaching staff came up with the "Junior Package." It is made up of about 20 plays in which Junior plays tight end or running back. The Chargers use the plays when they are near their opponent's goal line or need a few yards to make a first down. Junior's size, strength, speed, and sure hands help his team move the ball.

"I look at myself as a decoy," Junior told the *Columbus Dispatch*. "But if someone doesn't pay attention to me, we have something for that, too."

In 1999, Junior caught two passes for eight yards in regular-season action. He was his usual head-cracking self on defense. Before the Chargers took on the Cincinnati Bengals on September 19, Bengal head coach Bruce Coslet said, "I hope he plays the whole game at tight end and doesn't play linebacker. That would be nice, but I don't think it's going to happen."

It didn't. Junior made three tackles, had one sack, and recovered a fumble on the Bengal three-yard line. Junior's recovery led to a Charger field goal that cut the Bengals' lead to 7–3 in the first quarter. The Chargers went on to crush the Bengals, 34–7.

It is no surprise that Junior is one of the best — and most feared — linebackers in the history of the National Football League. Bobby Ross, who coached the Chargers from 1992 through 1996, thinks Junior will end up in the Pro Football Hall of Fame after he retires.

"The big difference between Junior and other great linebackers is his athletic ability and speed," Coach Ross told the *Chicago Tribune*. "You're talking about a player who is very, very quick and has great change of direction. He's an emotional player, but he is also a controlled player."

That emotion helps Junior excel.

ISLAND SON

Tiaina Seau, Jr. was born on January 19, 1969, in San Diego, California. His family is Samoan, and they moved back to American Samoa when Junior was a toddler. American Samoa is a group of islands in the South Pacific Ocean near New Zealand. He earned the nickname *Junior* because his father's name is Tiaina.

When Junior was five years old, his family moved back to the United States. They lived in Oceanside, California, about 30 miles north of the city of San Diego. Mr. Seau worked as a janitor and was a deacon at the local Samoan church. Junior's mom, Luisa, worked at laundromats and at a store on the nearby army base.

The house that the Seau family lived in was small, so Junior's three sisters and his parents shared the bedrooms while Junior and his two brothers, Savaii and Tony, slept in the garage. The garage had a cold concrete floor and a leaky roof. The boys used heaters to keep warm in the winter. Their beds were wedged between a dishwasher and a car. But they had old Motown soul records — Junior calls them "garage tunes" — to keep them happy and dancing.

Junior's neighborhood was ruled by gangs, drugs, and violence. His parents were very strict. They wanted to keep their kids out of trouble. Even so, Junior's younger brother Tony joined a gang and was later sent to jail for 10 years for being involved in a shooting.

"My childhood is a key to my success," Junior told the *Los Angeles Times*. "I learned how bad [life] could be."

At the same time, Junior says, his dad taught him about morals, values, and goals. Junior was already a natural athlete and a fiery competitor. He was good enough to play on the varsity teams in three high school sports: football, basketball, and track. His coaches were amazed at how intense Junior was and how hard he worked to succeed.

Dave Barrett, one of the football coaches at Oceanside High, remembers seeing Junior outside the weight room early one morning during summer vacation. "He was doing sprints, push-ups, sit-ups, all by himself," Coach Barrett told the *Los Angeles Times*. "I just stopped in amazement."

THE TWO-WAY TRADITION

Junior is not the first "two-way" linebacker in NFL history. Until the 1960s, many players played both defense and offense. They switched back and forth during games, participating *in almost every play!* The last to do it was linebacker/center Chuck Bednarik of the Philadelphia Eagles. Chuck, a Hall of Famer, retired in 1962.

MR. EVERYTHING

As a senior, Junior became the first player in North County's history to win Player of the Year honors in both football and basketball. In football, he had 123 tackles, 14 sacks, and five interceptions at linebacker. He also caught 71 passes for 1,115 yards and 15 touchdowns as a receiver. In basketball, he averaged 23 points per game and led his team to the league championship.

Junior was offered a football scholarship to the University of Southern California (USC). But he couldn't play during his freshman season (1987) because of a poor score on his

SEAU STUFF

Birth Date January 19, 1969

Height 6 feet 3 inches

Weight 250 lbs.

Home La Jolla, California

Here's Samoa When he was a kid, Junior's family spoke only Samoan at home. Junior did not learn English until he was seven years old. He and his brothers wore *lavalavas* (traditional Samoan skirts) at home, and learned the Samoan slap dance. Junior does a version of the slap dance to celebrate after he sacks a quarterback.

college-entrance exam. Junior spent the season in the weight room and the classroom. By the start of the 1988 season, no player on the team was stronger or more determined. But this time, Junior was hampered by injuries. He played only on special teams (punts, kickoffs, and field goals) and as a backup linebacker.

Junior's junior year was a different story. Healthy again, he was given a chance to start, and he ran wild!

He set a team sack record (19) and earned team MVP and All-America honors. He decided not to return to USC for his senior season. Instead, he entered the 1990 NFL draft and was thrilled when his hometown team, the San Diego Chargers, chose him fifth overall.

Junior smashed his way into the NFL during his rookie season, in 1990. He started 15 games and became the Chargers' second-leading tackler, with 85. In each of the next three seasons, he led the team in tackles and was chosen to play in the Pro Bowl.

Junior blossomed in 1994. He made a team-leading 155 tackles and was named the NFL's Linebacker of the Year. He also showed the heart of a champion.

During a November game, Junior suffered a pinched nerve in his neck. The injury often made his left arm numb and almost useless. Yet he refused to stop playing, and he led his team into the playoffs. In the AFC championship game, Junior made 16 tackles as the Chargers held the Pittsburgh Steelers to a measly 66 yards rushing and won, 17–13.

That performance sent the Chargers into the Super Bowl, against the San Francisco 49ers. Junior gave it all he had in the big game, racking up 11 tackles and a sack. But the Chargers met their match in 49er quarterback Steve Young. Steve threw a Super Bowl–record six touchdown passes as San Francisco won, 49–26. Even so, Junior had definitely become *The Man* in San Diego.

THE FIRE STILL BURNS

The Chargers have struggled since their 1994 Super Bowl appearance, but Junior's competitive fires still burn red–hot on game day. In 1999, he finished with a team–high 98 tackles, plus three and one half sacks, one interception, and one fumble recovery. He also helped out on offense and was honored as the Chargers' MVP and Defensive Player of the Year. The Chargers finished with a disappointing 8–8 record, but Junior was determined to do everything in his power to make the team a winner again.

"I'm afraid of being average," Junior told *Sports Illustrated.* "I have a real fear of being just another linebacker."

A GREAT DECADE

In 2000, Junior proved once again that he definitely was *not* "just another linebacker." His outstanding season included 122 tackles, three and one half sacks, and two pass interceptions. Junior was named to the NFL's All–Decade Team of the 1990s in recognition of his 11 seasons of outstanding play.

Despite Junior's standout year, the Chargers finished with a dismal 1–15 record. But during their horrendous season, Junior showed his class and determination. Even when San Diego was in danger of becoming the first NFL team to go 0–16, Junior put in his best effort on the field — often playing in pain. Junior went even further by signing a mid-season contract extension with the Chargers. Junior was sending the clear message to his teammates and the San Diego organization that he will be there when the team starts to turn around their fortunes.

In 2001, San Diego started their climb back into playoff contention. They went 5-11 as Junior racked up another 95 tackles.

Junior's off-field activities are plenty to applaud, too. In 1992, he established the Junior Seau Foundation, an organization that has awarded more than 200 college scholarships to college-bound students. Junior also shows his generous attitude towards kids every December when he takes 200 underprivileged youngsters on a Christmas shopping spree to buy gifts.

Junior's formula for success is simple. "I just go back to do what I believe, which is hard work. There's no secret to success; it's hard work," he says.

>> BRETT FAVRE

The three-time NFL MVP is at the top of his game

What kind of player wins three straight NFL MVP awards, successfully battles against addiction, wins a Super Bowl, and overcomes the disappointment of losing a possible second straight Super Bowl by only one touchdown? It's the kind of player with outstanding on-field skills and a personality built on integrity, honesty, and loyalty.

Quarterback Brett Favre of the Green Bay Packers is one of the NFL's greatest players of all time. He was voted as the ninth-best player in the "NFL Player of the Century" voting and was picked to the 1990s NFL All-Decade Second Team. Brett has built his reputation on an unmatched record of leadership, durability, productivity, and big-game performance.

THE BIG PLAY IN THE BIG GAME

January 26, 1996. Super Bowl XXXI: The Green Bay Packers are playing against the New England Patriots inside the Superdome in New Orleans, Louisiana.

It's the opening minutes of the first quarter and Green Bay has the ball on their own 46-yard line. Brett starts to call signals when he notices that the Patriot linebackers are getting ready to blitz — and it's only Green Bay's second play of the game! Brett had studied the films for days. He knows the early blitz by the Pats is intended to put the pressure on Green Bay right from the beginning of the game. He also knows that this play could be bigger than any play the Packers made all season.

Brett changes his call at the line of scrimmage: "74 Razor!" he shouts to his teammates. He drops back, looking for receiver Andre Rison to get open. He fires a bullet that Andre pulls in at New England's 20-yard line — and the speedy end duckwalks into the end zone for a 54-yard TD!

"I went bananas," Brett wrote in his autobiography, *Favre: For the Record.* Brett ripped off his helmet and starting celebrating as if it was the first TD pass he ever threw. Here was Brett, playing in the biggest game of his life — and making the biggest play of his life. His quick-thinking and on-target delivery got the Packers off to a quick start on their way to a 35–21 Super Bowl victory.

Later in the game, Brett found Antonio Freeman open for an 81-yard touchdown, the longest TD from scrimmage in Super Bowl history. Brett hit on 14 of 27 passes for 246 yards and two touchdowns that day. It was the highlight of a great career in which Brett had accomplished so much, while overcoming tremendous adversity.

DOWN ON THE BAYOU

Brett Lorenzo Favre was born on October 10, 1969 in Gulfport, Mississippi. He grew up in the town of Kiln [KILL] in southern Mississippi, about 12 miles from the Gulf of Mexico. Brett has two brothers — Scott and Jeff — and a younger sister, Brandi. Brett's mom taught special education at Hancock North Central High School. His dad, or "Big Irv," as Brett calls him, taught physical education and coached the football team at Hancock North Central. All three Favre boys played quarterback for their dad at Hancock.

The Favres were a tight family. "We grew up a close family, emotionally and physically. You could hardly swing a cat without hitting one of my relatives. Aunts, uncles, cousins — they all lived nearby," Brett says. Even Brett's grandmother, Mee–Maw, lived in the neighborhood.

Kiln is a very small town and the pace is slow. "There isn't much to see in Kiln. About all there is a yellow caution light surrounded by a few businesses. Mostly, we just have red clay roads that wind their way off into the backwoods," Brett says.

When Brett was one year old, he got his first football uniform. He enjoyed playing football with his dad and brothers as he was growing up. He played in his first organized football game in fifth grade. "I was really nervous before my first game. But once the game started, I settled down and scored three touchdowns!" Brett said.

At Hancock, Brett played baseball and football. But with his dad as the football coach, Brett preferred the action on the gridiron. He played quarterback, strong safety, punter, and was the place–kicker on the Hancock team. Playing for his dad was sometimes tough, but Brett didn't mind. "You get a lot more attention than you would if you were just another guy. I enjoyed that . . . I know my dad was tougher on me than he was on the other guys, but I was okay with that."

Brett attended Southern Mississippi University, playing under head coach Jim Carmody. When he joined Southern Miss in his freshman year, he was the seventh–string quarterback. But he worked hard and with some lucky breaks, he was soon the number–three play caller.

Before he knew it, Brett found himself in a game against Tulane, with his team losing, 17–3. On that day, he fashioned one of his soon–to–be famous come–from–behind victories. He rallied Southern Miss to a 31–24 win. From then on, Brett was his team's starting quarterback. As a freshman, he set a school record by throwing 15 TDs.

In his sophomore year, Brett led Southern Miss to a 10–2 record, including a 32–18 win over the University of Texas at El Paso in the Independence Bowl. He set single-season school records for passing yards (2,271), total offense yards (2,256), and touchdowns (16). Coach Curley Hallman, who replaced Jim Carmody, saw his quarterback's tremendous talent. "The mark of a truly great player is that he makes the other players around him look a little better. And Brett has that kind of quality about him," Coach Hallman said.

In the summer between his junior and senior years, Brett was in a car accident that almost cost him his life. Heading home from a fishing trip in July, his car went out of control, slid down an embankment, flipped three times in the air, and smashed into a tree. He had major surgery to repair his damaged intestines.

Brett recovered remarkably well and was soon back in action on the football field. He made an emotional return to his team in Southern Mississippi's second game of the season — against Alabama at Legion Field in Birmingham, Alabama. As Brett jogged onto to field, 86,000 'Bama fans started cheering for him. "When I got into the huddle, all of the [Southern Miss] guys had tears in their eyes. It was a great reception," Brett said. Alabama fans might have been glad to see him healthy and playing again, but they weren't too pleased when he led Southern Miss to a 31–24 victory over Alabama!

Southern Miss kept rolling up the wins as the season went on. The team finished with an 8-2 record and was selected to play in the All–American Bowl. Southern Miss lost to North Carolina State, 31–27, although Brett was named the game's MVP. He was also named to the East–West Shriner game and, once again, won game–MVP honors.

Brett finished his career at Southern Miss with school records for yards (8,193), pass attempts (1,234), completions (656), completion percentage (53.0), and TDs (55).

When the college draft rolled around, the Atlanta Falcons chose Brett as the 33rd pick. He was on his way to the pros.

EARLY LIFE IN THE PROS

Although he played pretty well in the Falcons' 1991 exhibition season (completing 14 of 34 passes for 160 yards and two touchdowns), Brett was the team's third-string quarterback behind Chris Miller and Billy Joe Tolliver by the time the season started. He got to play in only two games, completing no passes in five attempts, and throwing two interceptions.

Many people thought that Brett hurt his chances of getting more playing time in Atlanta because he enjoyed the party life too much. He would sometimes show up late for team practices. After the 1991 season, the Falcons traded Brett to the Green Bay Packers.

Brett started the 1992 season as backup to Packer starting quarterback Don Majkowski. But in the third game of the season, Don was injured and Brett was called on to fill in. All he did was fire a 35-yard game-winning TD to receiver Kitrick Taylor with 13 seconds left in the game! That performance earned Brett the starter's role. He started 13 games and was named to his first Pro Bowl. The Packers ended the season with a 9-7 record.

A TOUGH PLAYBOOK

"For the next two and a half seasons, from 1992 through the midway point of 1994, we had our moments," Brett said about the Packers. The Green Bay offense was a very complicated system of hundreds of plays. Brett found the play calling tough to master. "I struggled and struggled for a long time," he said. Green Bay head coach Mike Holmgren expected a lot from his talented young quarterback and pushed Brett hard to meet those expectations. Coach Holmgren would yell, curse, and complain to motivate Brett. "Let the system work for you!" he often hollered at him.

The Packers finished the 1993 season at 9–7. It was the first time the team had back–to–back winning seasons since 1966 and 1967. The Packers won a wild–card playoff game against the Detroit Lions, 28–24, but lost the division championship game to the Dallas Cowboys, 27–24. Brett had another solid season and was once again picked for the Pro Bowl.

THE TURNAROUND

"I rolled into the 1994 season convinced we were going to be really good," Brett said. He was right, but Green Bay went through some hard times before they turned things around for good.

Through the first six games of the 1994 season, Brett would have one great game, then a bad one. He was still learning and making mistakes. Finally, in the seventh game of the season, against the Minnesota Vikings, Brett and his teammates hit rock bottom. Brett got hurt in the first quarter and was replaced by Mark Brunell (now with the Jacksonville Jaguars). At halftime, Brett told Coach Holmgren that he was feeling well enough to go back into the game. But Coach Holmgren told Brett that he was staying with Mark. Brett was crushed. The Packers lost, 13–10, in overtime and their record dropped to 3–4.

Brett thought that he had blown his chance of being the Packers number one quarterback. He thought that Mark would be the starter for the rest of the season. Fortunately, Green Bay quarterback coach Steve Mariucci had a lot of confidence in Brett. He convinced Coach Holmgren to stick with Brett. Brett went home after the loss to the Vikings to think things over. "I did a lot of soul-searching and when I came back I had one goal: I was going to be the best quarterback in the NFL," Brett said.

That's exactly what happened. Brett took charge on the field and led the Packers to seven wins in their last 10 games, including a wild-card playoff victory over the Lions, 16–12. The Packers once again lost to Dallas in the division title game, but Brett's team had become one of the league's most respected. Coach Holmgren's decision to stick with Brett had paid off.

In 1995, Brett threw for 38 TDs and a league-leading 4,413 yards. He won his first NFL MVP award. Green Bay went 11–5 to win their division. They headed into the playoffs on a roll. First Green Bay knocked off Atlanta, 27–20, in a wild-card game and then beat the defending Super Bowl champion San Francisco 49ers, 27–17, in the division title game. But *once again*, Dallas knocked out Green Bay's dream of a Super Bowl title by topping them, 38–27, in the NFC title game.

DARK SECRET

On the field Brett had come to be considered one of the NFL's top players. But off the field Brett had a secret problem that was slowly tearing him apart. He had become addicted to painkilling pills and couldn't stop taking them. The life of an NFL player is filled with painful injuries. Brett wanted to keep playing even when he was injured. So he began taking pills to dull the pain. The more his body hurt, the more pills he took — even in the off-season.

In February 1996, Brett suffered a seizure after surgery on his left ankle. His head, arms, and legs shook uncontrollably. That's when he knew he had an addiction problem.

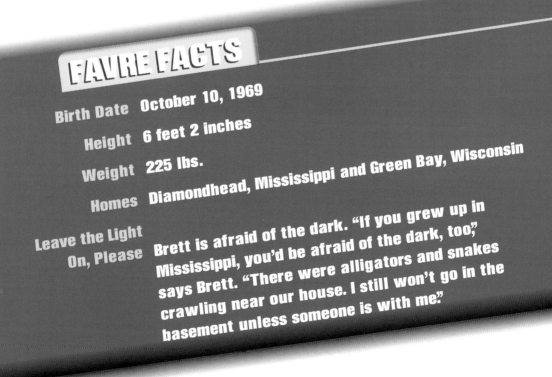

FAVRE FACTS

Birth Date October 10, 1969

Height 6 feet 2 inches

Weight 225 lbs.

Homes Diamondhead, Mississippi and Green Bay, Wisconsin

Leave the Light On, Please Brett is afraid of the dark. "If you grew up in Mississippi, you'd be afraid of the dark, too," says Brett. "There were alligators and snakes crawling near our house. I still won't go in the basement unless someone is with me."

By then, many friends and family had figured out that Brett had a serious problem. In May 1996, Brett entered the Menninger Clinic in Topeka, Kansas to kick his addiction. His 45-day stay at the clinic was no picnic: Brett had to take a deep look at himself and come to grips with the fact that he *was* a drug addict. It was a painful journey that he made successfully. Finally, in late June, doctors told him that he was ready to go home.

Before the season began, Brett married his long-time girlfriend, Deanna. Brett and Deanna's daughter, Britanny, attended their wedding. Britanny was born to the couple in Brett's sophomore year at college. The three were finally together as a family. With his personal problems behind him and a supportive family by his side, Brett was ready to leap into the 1996 season.

THE MAGIC SEASON

"We were here for only one reason: to win the Super Bowl . . . I think everyone agreed. We had enough talent," Brett said at the beginning of training camp.

The Packers displayed that talent early. They outscored their opponents, 110–11, in the first three games of the season. They kept piling up wins as the season rolled on. On offense, Green Bay scored more points than any team in the league. On defense, they allowed the fewest points. The Packers finished at 13–3 and Brett clearly established himself as one of the game's greats. His 39 touchdown passes set an NFC record for most TDs in a single season.

He also threw for an NFL–best 3,899 yards. Once again, he was voted the NFL MVP.

Green Bay's road to the Super Bowl took them through a division title win over San Francisco, 35–14, and a 30–13 NFC championship–game pounding of the Carolina Panthers. The victorious showdown against the New England Patriots in Super Bowl XXXI was the perfect ending to a sensational 1996 season.

"The Super Bowl was one of my most enjoyable games ever," said Brett in his autobiography. "I felt so clear and so at ease, it was like when you hear about Michael Jordan being in a zone and never missing. Well, that's the way I felt."

ROLLING IN THE YEARS

Brett won his third straight MVP award in 1997, after leading the Pack to another 13–3 season. No one in the history of the NFL had ever won three straight. "Each of the MVPs represents something different," Brett said. "The first one was like 'Okay, you've arrived. You're established.' The second MVP was like 'I told you so.' To me it represents an ability to overcome. I came back clean and healthy from my addiction. The third MVP represents consistency."

The Packers went to the Super Bowl again, but came up short this time, losing to the Denver Broncos, 31–24.

In 1998, Brett led the NFL is completions (347) and passing yards (4,212). The Packers went 11–5. They were edged by the 49ers in the division title game, 30–27. There would not be a third straight trip to the Super Bowl.

COOL, CALM, COLLECTING

Brett has saved his game jerseys from every team he's played for. He has jerseys from high school, college, and the pros. He also has his jerseys from college-bowl games, Pro Bowl games, and the Super Bowl.

The Packers slipped to 8–8 in 1999, but rebounded to a 9–7 record in 2000. In February 2001, Brett signed a lifetime contract with the Packers, almost assuring that he will finish his career in Green Bay. Packer general manager and head coach Mike Sherman called Brett's signing "historic." "I do not think there is a player in the NFL that experiences a relationship with the fans like Brett Favre does. That's very, very special," said Coach Sherman.

The Packers reemerged as one of the league's top teams in 2001, posting a 12–4 record. Brett had another solid season, throwing for 3,921 yards and 32 TDs. Green Bay beat San Francisco in the wild–card playoff game, 25–15, but got clobbered by the St. Louis Rams, 45–17, in the division title game. Brett threw six interceptions in the disappointing loss. Green Bay's strong 2001 performance behind their 32-year old quarterback put other teams on notice that they were back and aiming for another shot at a Super Bowl victory in the future.

Brett's career performance has him on a sure path to the NFL Hall of Fame. In addition to his three straight MVPs and the Super Bowl win, take a look at some of Brett's career highlights going into the 2002 season:

- Brett tops all NFL quarterbacks in completions, pass attempts, passing yards, and TDs in the decade of 1991–2000.

- Brett is the only quarterback in NFL history to throw for 3,000 yards in 10 straight seasons.

- Brett owns the NFL record for quarterbacks by starting in 157 consecutive games.

- Brett has six 30-touchdown seasons — the most in NFL history.

"In my mind, I think I can be the best ever. That's my goal, to be the best. I don't know if that will ever happen, but I think it's important to set high goals," Brett wrote in *For the Record*. "I want someone to write a book someday and say, 'That Brett Favre was the greatest quarterback of all time. He could do it all,'" Brett wrote.

>> EDDIE GEORGE

**No one eats up yards
and scares tacklers like
"The Beast"**

When the going gets tough, the Tennessee Titans unleash The Beast. That's their 6-foot-3-inch, 240-pound monster running back, Eddie George, who may be the strongest, toughest running back in the NFL.

The Beast is a bruiser who averaged more than 300 carries per season in each of his first six NFL seasons. He can power his team with his mighty legs like few other backs in the league. Opponents know that to stop the Titans, they have to stop The Beast.

"I don't like tackling him," cornerback Ashley Ambrose of the New Orleans Saints told the *Tennesseean*. "A guy like that gets in the secondary, he's what, two hundred and forty pounds? Look at me. I weigh one hundred and eighty pounds. I'm trying to bring that guy down by myself, and it's tough."

The Beast can turn a game around by himself. On January 16, 2000, the Titans were trailing the Indianapolis Colts, 9–6, in the third quarter of the AFC divisional playoff game. It was second down, and the Titans had

the ball on their own 32-yard line. Quarterback Steve McNair handed off to The Beast. Eddie roared through a hole in the Colt defensive line, cut back, and headed for open field. He charged downfield with three Colts hot on his heels. At the Colt 40-yard line, The Beast kicked into another gear and pulled away from them.

The Beast fought off a defender's desperate attempt to strip the ball out of his arms, and plowed into the end zone. Touchdown! The Beast had rumbled 68 yards to put the Titans ahead, 12–9.

The Beast gobbled up big chunks of ground for the rest of the game, finishing with 162 yards rushing. The Titans won, 19–16. The Beast was a beauty that day!

MAMA'S BEAST

After the game, The Beast got a big, warm hug from his mom, who started to cry because she was so happy.

"Oh, Mama," Eddie said softly. "Stop that. Don't cry."

"You made me so proud!" she cried. "And you scored a touchdown!"

"Got to do it again, Mama," Eddie said.

And he did. The following week, in the AFC championship game against the Jacksonville Jaguars, The Beast cranked out 105 total yards rushing and receiving. The Titans stormed to a 33–14 victory.

The Beast was awesome again in the Super Bowl a week later. He scored two key touchdowns against the St. Louis Rams in the second half to help the Titans claw their way back into the game after trailing, 16–0. The Titans tied the

A SWEET ROLE MODEL

One of Eddie's role models was running back Walter Payton. He played 13 seasons for the Chicago Bears and retired in 1987 as the NFL's all-time leading rusher, with 16,726 yards. Walter was nicknamed Sweetness because of his graceful running and sweet personality. "I want to understand his work ethic, what it took him to get to the top," says Eddie.

score, 16–16, in the fourth quarter, but the Rams managed to win the game, 23–16, after Tennessee's final drive ended one yard short of a touchdown as time ran out. But Eddie — and his mom — had much to be proud of.

THE DREAM UNDER THE CHRISTMAS TREE

Eddie Nathan George was born on September 24, 1973, in Philadelphia, Pennsylvania. He and his older sister, Leslie, were raised by their mom, Donna George, after their parents were divorced. She was a production manager for Ford Aerospace and, later, worked as an airline flight attendant.

Eddie had sky-high plans of his own. When he was only eight years old, he told his mom that he wanted to have the Heisman Trophy under the family Christmas tree someday. The Heisman is awarded each year to the best college football player in the United States. Eddie's mom thought it was an awfully big present to wish for. But the seed of a dream had been planted in Eddie's heart. If it hadn't been for his mom, his dream might have been destroyed.

FORK IN THE ROAD

Eddie grew up in a rough part of Philadelphia. He was disrespectful and lazy during his early years at Abington High School. He didn't want to study. He wanted to play football and listen to his Walkman instead. When he was 15, Eddie earned such poor grades and was so wild that his mom grew very concerned. She was afraid that he would fall in with a bad group of friends and get involved with drugs, alcohol, and crime. Something had to be done.

Eddie's mom decided to send him to Fork Union Military Academy, in Fork Union, Virginia, for his junior and senior years of high school. Eddie was stunned.

"He said, 'Why are you doing this to me?'" Eddie's mom says. "I said, 'It's what I have to do if you want to fulfill your dreams and goals.'"

Eddie and his mom were both in tears the day he left. When he got to Fork Union, his football coach told him that he could achieve anything he wanted in life if he just changed his attitude. The academy's early-morning wake-up calls, tiring physical drills, and tough rules did the trick. Eddie became a new person. He learned to follow the rules and do what was expected of him. When it came to physical fitness, he did even more. Eddie became a regular fitness freak.

Working hard became a way of life for Eddie. After he joined the Titans, his coaches and teammates raved about how hard he worked at staying in shape. He would jump on a stationary bike or run extra sprints whenever there was some downtime during practice. He became a perfectionist who would do whatever it takes to be the best. "Eddie hates making mistakes," said Titan coach Jeff Fisher. "It's part of his competitive drive."

BUCKEYE MENACE

After his junior and senior years at Fork Union, Eddie took his fierce work ethic to Ohio State University in 1992. He did not become a starter on the football team until his junior season, but he kept working hard so that he would be ready when he got his chance.

Was Eddie ever ready. During his junior season, in 1994, he gained 1,442 yards and earned the nickname The Beast for his size and ferocious, punishing running style. In 1995, he was even better. The Buckeyes won their first 11 games. Rival players and coaches watched in awe, saying they had never seen a running back like him: a big bruiser who could run like the wind.

In one game, The Beast chewed up the University of Illinois, which had one of the top defenses against the run. He set a school record of 314 rushing yards and scored twice in a 41–3 victory.

"He was awesome," said Illinois defensive coordinator Denny Marcin. "I've coached thirty-two years and have not seen a back like that. I hope not to see one again."

That season, Eddie rushed for 100 yards, or more, in every game. He ended up with 1,826 yards on 303 carries. He also caught 44 passes, for 399 yards, and scored 24 touchdowns. He was rewarded with the Christmas present he had wanted as an eight-year-old: the Heisman Trophy.

With the Heisman safely tucked under his arm, Eddie was picked 14th overall in the first round of the NFL draft by the Houston Oilers in April 1996. (The Oilers became the Tennessee Titans in 1999.)

The Beast felt right at home in the NFL. He rushed for 1,368 yards and was the league's Rookie-of-the-Year. In 1997, he earned his first Pro Bowl appearance. He rushed for more than 1,300 yards in each of his next three seasons.

Eddie had a huge season in 1999, racking up 1,304 rushing yards and another 458 receiving yards. Before the AFC divisional playoff game against the Colts, Coach Fisher took Eddie aside and told him, "This is why we drafted you. To win big games like this."

The Beast's grinding, punishing runs were the key to the Titans' victory over the Colts and their trip to the Super Bowl. The world of football had learned to fear The Beast.

"This has been my best season as far as what they have asked me to do," Eddie told reporters before the Super Bowl. "But my real breakout year — I don't think that's happened yet. I haven't had that big year yet."

A YEAR TO REMEMBER

That big year came in 2000. Eddie set career highs with 1,509 rushing yards, 403 carries, 14 touchdowns, and 50 receptions. By rushing for at least 1,200 yards in each of his first five seasons, Eddie joined Eric Dickerson as the only player in NFL history to accomplish the feat.

The Titans finished the 2000 season with a division-leading record of 13-3. In the playoffs, Tennessee lost to the Baltimore

Ravens, 24–10, in a first-round playoff matchup. Eddie had a solid game with 91 rushing yards and eight receptions.

In the off-season, Eddie got his college degree in landscape architecture from Ohio State University. Since 2000, Eddie had been putting in long hours of study to reach his goal of graduation.

Expectations for Eddie and the Titans were high for the 2001 season. Unfortunately, the Titans were only able to put together a 7–9 record, tying them with the Cleveland Browns for third place in their division. Eddie was bothered by ankle and toe problems, and failed to rush for at least 1,000 yards for the first time in his career. He finished with 939 rushing yards and only five rushing TDs. Although it was a very disappointing season, The Beast will surely be back in top form in 2002.

You'll probably start to feel the ground rumbling once again.

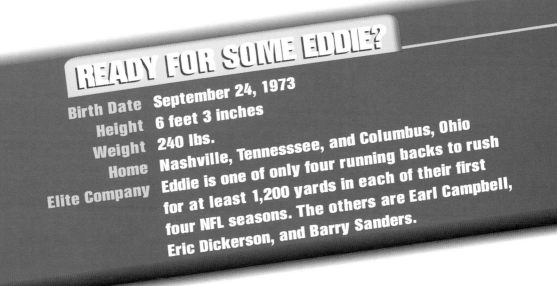

READY FOR SOME EDDIE?

Birth Date September 24, 1973
Height 6 feet 3 inches
Weight 240 lbs.
Home Nashville, Tennesssee, and Columbus, Ohio
Elite Company Eddie is one of only four running backs to rush for at least 1,200 yards in each of their first four NFL seasons. The others are Earl Campbell, Eric Dickerson, and Barry Sanders.

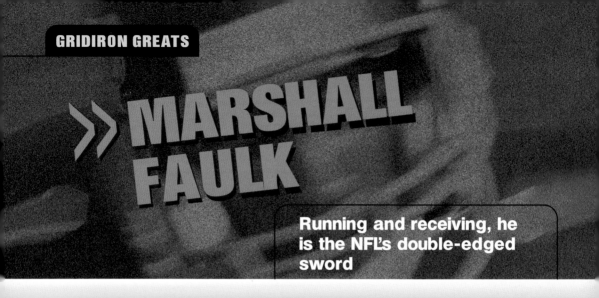

>> MARSHALL FAULK

Running and receiving, he is the NFL's double-edged sword

On December 26, 1999, the St. Louis Rams were battling the Chicago Bears at the Trans World Dome, in St. Louis, Missouri. After the first period, the score was still 0–0. The Rams' monster offense just couldn't get anything going against the tough Bear defense until. . .

With eight minutes 36 seconds left in the first half, St. Louis had the ball. On second down at the Chicago 48-yard line, the Rams' Marshall Faulk caught a short pass over his shoulder as he darted toward the right sideline. Then he outraced the Bear defenders for a touchdown. The Rams were on their way to a 34–12 victory.

Marshall had 12 receptions for a whopping 204 yards that day. His big day took him over 1,000 receiving yards for the season. Only the best receivers in the NFL gain that many yards in a season.

But Marshall is not a receiver. He's a running back. In fact, he's an All-Pro running back who also rushed for more than 1,000 yards in 1999. In the game against the

Bears, Marshall became only the second running back in NFL history to gain more than 1,000 yards rushing and 1,000 yards receiving in the same season. (Roger Craig of the San Francisco 49ers did it in 1985.)

Marshall's dazzling running and receiving make him one of the most feared offensive weapons in the NFL. When the Rams played the Tennessee Titans in the 2000 Super Bowl, Marshall was held to only 17 yards rushing by the tough Tennessee defense. But the Titans couldn't stop him from catching passes. He ended up with five catches for 90 yards to help the Rams win, 23–16.

"He always amazes me," Ram quarterback Kurt Warner told reporters that season. "He's just a special guy once he gets the ball. There are a lot of times I find myself just sitting back and watching him."

When he's carrying the ball, Marshall is as slippery as an eel. He senses where tacklers are and takes off at the last second, leaving them grasping nothing but air. "It's like Marshall has eyes in the back of his head," Ram running-back coach Wilbert Montgomery told *Sports Illustrated*.

Before the Super Bowl, reporters asked Marshall why he's so good. He replied, "I can see everything. I'm aware of what's going on. I know a lot about football and what everybody is supposed to be doing."

Each week, Marshall studies the strategies that opposing defenses are likely to use. He is a great listener. He takes pride in remembering lessons taught by his coaches. Marshall has always been fascinated by the X's and O's on the coach's chalkboard. That is a good thing because

THE MARSHALL PLAN

The Marshall Faulk Foundation helps kids in poor city neighborhoods like the one in which Marshall grew up. He donated $500,000 to the foundation when he joined the Rams, in 1999. Each time he scores a touchdown, he gives $2,000 to The Marshall Plan to help inner-city kids.

his love of football and his ability to use his mind helped Marshall escape a dangerous childhood that could have brought him down before he ever got started.

MEAN STREETS

Marshall William Faulk was born on February 26, 1973, in New Orleans, Louisiana. He grew up with his parents and five older brothers in one of the absolute worst neighborhoods in New Orleans. Violence and drugs ruled the scene. It was like a war zone.

"I had a guy pull a gun on me," said Marshall. "Shooting, guys dying from crack, that was just part of life. It prepared me for other obstacles in my life that I had to overcome."

Marshall's dad, Roosevelt, was rarely at home. He was busy running a restaurant and working for a trucking company. Marshall's mom, Cecile, worked odd jobs while trying to raise her six sons. Marshall's five brothers got into trouble. He lost friends to guns and drugs.

Marshall was lucky that people always seemed to look out for him. In grade school, one of his teachers, Mrs. Porter, helped keep him out of trouble.

"Mrs. Porter reported to my mom on how I was doing in school," says Marshall. "If my grades were bad or if I misbehaved in school, I couldn't play football that week. Mrs. Porter made me miss a lot of games."

At George Washington Carver High School, Marshall's football coach, Wayne Reese, also looked out for him. Coach Reese knew Marshall had the potential to go far in professional sports.

HANGING IN THERE

At one point in high school, Marshall decided to quit football so he could get a job and make some money. Coach Reese told him that a great future lay ahead if he could just hang tough and strive for it. He got Marshall a job as a janitor at the school. The job helped Marshall continue to play football and stay in school.

Coach Reese made his players practice before and after school so that they would be too pooped to get into trouble after they left for the day. Somehow, Marshall still found enough time to study football closely and to analyze plays.

Marshall became such a fine all-round player that he played kicker, quarterback, wide receiver, cornerback, and running back for Carver High. During his junior and senior seasons, Marshall rushed for 1,800 yards and scored

32 touchdowns. He also intercepted an impressive 11 passes on defense. Scouts from major colleges wanted him only as a defensive back. Marshall wanted to play running back.

"You get your mind set, and you stick with it," Marshall said. "I'm a firm believer that whatever I want to do, I'm going to do."

So Marshall decided to attend the first college that wanted him as a running back: San Diego State University.

Marshall was listed as the sixth-string running back when he arrived at San Diego State. That meant there were five running backs who would get to play before he did. Marshall changed that in a hurry. He moved up to second-string by impressing his coaches in pre-season practices.

Then, when the team's starting running back was hurt, Marshall got a chance to show what he could do. In only his second game, he set a national college rushing record of 386 yards and scored seven touchdowns. Marshall went on to become the first freshman running back to lead the nation in rushing (1,429 yards).

Marshall won All-America honors and finished in the Top 10 in the voting for the Heisman Trophy in each of his three seasons at San Diego State. When he decided to enter the 1994 NFL draft after his junior season, the Indianapolis Colts made him the second player chosen.

THE FUTURE ARRIVES

Marshall took the NFL by storm as a rookie. After three quarters of his very first game, against the Houston Oilers, Marshall had rushed for 143 yards and scored three TDs.

A MARSHALL MINUTE

Birth Date February 26, 1973

Height 5 feet 10 inchees

Weight 211 lbs.

Home St. Louis, Missouri

College major Public Administration

Favorite Sport to Play
(other than football) Golf

MR. SLEEPY As game time approaches, many NFL players start to get nervous or excited. Not Marshall. His eyelids grow heavy and he begins to let out loud yawns!

In his next game, against the Tampa Bay Buccaneers, he rushed for 104 yards and became the first rookie since 1980 to begin his NFL career with two 100-yard games. The great future Coach Reese predicted for Marshall had arrived.

"You better bring your track shoes and your lunch box to play him," said linebacker Darryl Talley of the Buffalo Bills. "You've got to chase him on first down and on second down, and then on third down he'll catch a pass out of the backfield. When do you ever get a break from this guy?"

After rushing for 1,282 yards, Marshall was chosen as the 1994 Offensive Rookie of the Year. Then he set an NFL record by rushing for 180 yards in the Pro Bowl. He was the only rookie in the game, but he was named the game's MVP.

"I've surprised myself," he said. "No one comes into the NFL and is able to do all the things I've done this fast. It scares me to know I'm being so successful so early. When I learn all the things I need to learn, how good can I be?"

In 1998, his fifth season with the Colts, Marshall led the NFL in total yards and was selected to his third Pro Bowl. But his contract with the Colts was up after the season. The team decided to save money by drafting a young running back and trading Marshall. They sent him to the St. Louis Rams, who had had an awful 4–12 record in 1998 and looked as if they were going absolutely nowhere.

Marshall was upset about the trade, but when he went to a Rams' camp to check out his new teammates, he found a group of talented offensive players, such as wide receivers Isaac Bruce, Torry Holt, Ricky Proehl, and Az–Zahir Hakim.

With Marshall joining the offense, the 1999 Rams became the biggest surprise of the season. Marshall broke the NFL all–purpose yardage record for one season with 1,381 rushing yards and 1,048 receiving yards, for a total of 2,429 yards. He was named the 1999 NFL Offensive Player of the Year and earned his fourth trip to the Pro Bowl in six seasons. He also helped the Rams win the Super Bowl.

As Kurt Warner said after the game, "The guy is phenomenal."

YOU CAN'T CATCH ME

Phenomenal — and then some. Marshall continued to keep opposing NFL defenders shaking in their boots during the 2000 season.

Marshall played in 14 of 16 games, but he rushed for 1,359 yards and scored a career-high 18 rushing touchdowns. The sure-handed running back added 81 receptions for 830 yards and eight touchdowns. Marshall was named to his fifth Pro Bowl. His best performance was against the New Orleans Saints in the final game of the regular season. He torched the Saints for 220 rushing yards, seven receptions, and three touchdowns. The Rams won the game, 26–21.

The Rams posted a 10–6 record on the season. They were knocked out of the playoffs in a wild-card game against the Saints, 31–28. Marshall was held to a season-low 24 rushing yards.

The Rams were determined to get back to the Super Bowl in 2001. Led by quarterback Kurt Warner, St. Louis tore through their opposition, posting a league-leading 14–2 record. The Rams' explosive offense scored 503 points — 90 points more than the second-highest scoring team, the Indianapolis Colts.

Marshall had yet another great season in 2001. He rushed for 1,382 yards, caught 83 passes, and scored 21 touchdowns. Marshall became the only player in NFL history with four 2000–plus yard seasons (rushing and receiving yards combined). He was he selected to his sixth

Pro Bowl. Marshall was edged out by teammate Kurt Warner for the league's MVP by only four points.

In the playoffs, the Rams crushed the Green Bay Packers, 45–17, in a first-round game. St. Louis then beat the Philadelphia Eagles, 29–24, in the conference championship game. Marshall went wild, rushing for 159 yards — a career-high playoff record — and scoring two touchdowns. Marshall knew it was one of his best games ever. "I left it all out there. I couldn't have written a script better than this," he said of his great performance and the team victory.

Once again, the Rams were headed to the Super Bowl. Their opponent would be the New England Patriots. Super Bowl XXXVI, played in Marshall's hometown, New Orleans, Louisiana, would be one to remember. The Patriots shocked the football world with a 20–17 victory over the heavily-favored Rams. And they did it on the most dramatic field goal in Super Bowl history. With no time left on the game clock, Pats' kicker Adam Vinatieri kicked a 48–yard field goal to give New England its first NFL title. It was an amazing finish to one of the finest Super Bowl games ever played.

Marshall didn't have the game he was hoping for in front of his hometown fans. The Patriot defense bottled him up, allowing him only 76 yards on 17 carries. The disappointing finish to another great season will surely be an incentive for him to drive the Ram offense in 2002.

GLOSSARY

adversity continued misfortune

architecture the art and occupation of designing
buildings and landscapes

caliber degree of value or worth

decoy someone or something used to draw attention
away from another

excel to do better than others

franchise a professional sports team

raved to have spoken with enthusiasm and praise

seizure a sudden attack where body parts shake
uncontrollably

RESOURCES

BOOKS

Bernstein, Ross. *Randy Moss: Star Wide Receiver.* Berkely Heights, NJ: Enslow Publishers, 2002.

Clark, Peter J., and Dale Ratermann. *101 Fun Facts About Kurt Warner.* Champaign, IL: Sports Publishing, 2000.

Favre, Brett, and Chris Havel. *Favre: For the Record.* New York, NY: Doubleday, 1997.

Rains, Bob. *Marshall Faulk: Rushing to Glory.* Champaign, IL: Sports Publishing, 1999.

Rekela, George. *Brett Favre: Star Quarterback.* Berkely Heights, NJ: Enslow Publishers, 2000.

Stewart, Mark. *Drew Bledsoe: Stand and Deliver.* Danbury, CT: Children's Press, 2000.

Stewart, Mark. *Steve McNair: Running and Gunning.* Brookfield, CT: Millbrook Press, 2001.

Trotter, Jim. *Junior Seau: Overcoming the Odds.* Champaign, IL: Sports Publishing, 2000.

>> RESOURCES

MAGAZINE

Sports Illustrated For Kids
135 W. 50th Street
New York, NY 10020
(800) 992–0196
http://www.sikids.com

WEB SITES

The Official Site of the National Football League
http://www.nfl.com
Learn about your favorite teams and players on this site.
Check out all of the up–to–the–minute scores, standings, and
statistics.

The Sporting News Online: NFL
http://www.sportingnews.com/nfl
Follow your favorite teams and players throughout the season
on this informative site.

>> RESOURCES

Yahoo! Sports: National Football League
http://sports.yahoo.com/nfl
Find out the latest NFL news on this site. Listen to broadcast events and visit the photo gallery.

SPORTS ILLUSTRATED FOR KIDS
http://www.sikids.com
Check out the latest sports news, cool games, and much more.